CCSS **Genre** Realistic F

Essential Question
How do writers look at success in different ways?

Try, Try Again

by Paul Mason

illustrated by
Juan Caminador

Chapter 1
The New Bike

A week had passed since Jerome's birthday, and he still hadn't ridden his new bike. His older brother Louis spied it hiding in a corner of the garage with the bow still dangling from the handlebars.

Louis found Jerome lying on his bed surrounded by a pile of comics.

"Hey," Jerome said. "What's up?"

"Your bike," Louis said, sitting on his bed. "I just noticed you haven't taken it out for a ride yet."

Jerome sighed, "What's the point of taking it out if I don't know how to ride it?"

"The point is you *learn*," Louis laughed. "You've heard that word before?"

"Ha, ha, very funny," Jerome said, giving him a playful shove.

"Seriously, I'm happy to teach you. We can work on it together since Mom and Dad are so busy at the moment."

Jerome thought for a moment and frowned. "I have been feeling bad that I can't ride my bike," he admitted. "Okay, when do we start?"

"How about right now? Let's go get the bike out of the garage," said Louis.

Louis took off all the wrapping paper and wheeled the bike out onto the long driveway.

He looked around the yard while Jerome strapped on his helmet. It was mostly flat. There was plenty of space for Jerome to learn, as long as he stayed away from the flower beds.

STOP AND CHECK

Why hasn't Jerome ridden his new bike?

4

Chapter 2

Lesson Over

Louis held the bike steady while Jerome sat on the seat. Jerome's feet almost reached the ground.

"Okay, here's what I want you to do," Louis said with authority. "I'm going to give you a push, and you're going to hold on and try to keep steady. Then start pedaling."

Jerome raised his eyebrows.

"A push? Are you sure?"

"Trust me, you'll be fine," said Louis. "Are you ready?"

Jerome tensed his shoulders. "I guess so," he said, gripping the handlebars.

Louis held onto Jerome's shoulder and started pushing him, the bike wheels spinning like tops. Jerome gathered speed. With a grunt, Louis gave his brother a final push, sending him racing down the driveway.

Jerome's arms wobbled, the handlebars wobbled, the bike wobbled, and he began to lose control. Thump! Jerome tumbled off the bike and sprawled onto the grass. Louis raced over to him.

Jerome picked himself up. He rubbed his elbow and brushed dirt from his knees.

"That was your great plan to teach me how to ride?" he asked angrily.

Louis felt guilty. "I'm really sorry. That wasn't supposed to happen."

"No, it wasn't," Jerome grumbled. "This lesson is over!"

Louis picked the bike up.

"Look, I realize now it wasn't a good idea to launch you like that," he admitted, "but don't give up yet. Let's try again, but this time, we'll take it step by step."

Jerome glared at him. "Maybe tomorrow," he said half-heartedly.

STOP AND CHECK

Why does Jerome glare at his brother?

Chapter 3

Learning to Ride

After school the next day, Louis and Jerome took the bike out again. This time Louis stayed by Jerome's side, hovering behind him, ready to catch him if he fell.

He taught him how to keep his balance, how to use the brakes, and how to put his feet down when he came to a stop.

For the rest of that week, they practiced every day. Little by little, Jerome's confidence grew as he learned to pedal and steer at the same time. It wasn't easy, but they were making progress.

"I want to ride on my own," Jerome said one day. "I want to give it another try. No shoving this time," he said.

"Sure," said Louis, "if you think you're ready." He stood back and watched as Jerome set off, shakily at first, then slowly gathered speed. Jerome pedaled along the driveway, wobbling just a little.

Jerome reached the end of the driveway.

"I'm going to turn around," he called to his brother.

But when he tried to turn, he lost his balance and fell into a heap on the grass.

Louis ran over. "Are you okay?" he asked.

Jerome gave him the thumbs-up. "I'm fine. Did you see? I rode all by myself!" He stood up and brushed himself off.

Louis beamed. He was really proud of his brother.

Despite the tumbles, Jerome hadn't given up but had kept trying to attain his goal of riding the bike on his own.

"I think you're ready to show Mom and Dad," said Louis.

STOP AND CHECK

Why is Jerome pleased with himself?

Chapter 4
Triumph

Jerome kept practicing while Louis set up two lawn chairs in the yard and then went to get their parents. Jerome was hiding in the garage, helmet on, ready to ride. He couldn't wait!

"What is it?" asked their mom with a suspicious look on her face. "What's the big surprise?"

"You'll see," said Louis with a wink.

"The day you help me cut the lawn without me asking, now *that* would be a surprise," his dad teased.

"You'll like this even better," promised Louis.

Facing the house, Louis raised his hand and then dropped it. That was the signal for Jerome to start pedaling. Mom and Dad turned to see Jerome wobbling his way out of the garage. Along the driveway he went, his face frozen in concentration, his legs rapidly pedaling, his hands locked onto the handlebars.

"Way to go, Jerome!" his mom called as she and his dad grinned at each other.

Jerome reached the end of the driveway. Then he turned around and came back down the driveway. He even managed a little wave.

Jerome did another lap around the driveway, then he braked and came to a stop. "Ta-daaa!" he said with a laugh, raising his arms in triumph.

His mom and dad clapped enthusiastically. "Now that *was* a nice surprise," said his dad. "When did you learn how to ride a bike, Jerome?"

"Louis taught me," he smiled.

"Jerome kept practicing," Louis pointed out, "even though it was hard at first and he fell over a few times."

"Good for you, Jerome," said his mom. "As I always say, if at first you don't succeed..."

"...try, try again," Jerome finished.

STOP AND CHECK

What does Jerome do to show he has learned to ride the bike?

Respond to Reading

Use the most important details from *Try, Try Again* to summarize the story. Your graphic organizer may help.

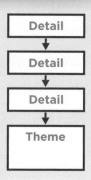

Text Evidence

1. What features of the story help you identify it as realistic fiction? GENRE

2. What is the theme of this story? How does Jerome's achievement help you figure out the theme? THEME

3. Jerome is "gripping the handlebars" on page 5. How does this show what Jerome is feeling? CONNOTATION AND DENOTATION

4. Write about how Jerome became successful at riding his bike. Use details from the story in your answer. WRITE ABOUT READING

Compare Texts

Read about a person who remembers what it was like to learn to ride a bike.

Sunlight Sparkling on Chrome

Like a river, the path ran before her;
To ride it she'd made up her mind.
Brave wheels went around and around,
Leaving her home behind.

Never before had she been this far,
To ride so steady, so right.
Brave wheels went around and around;
The handlebars were held tight.

She remembered the falls, the scratches,
Medals of her labor to learn.
Brave wheels went around and around,
Falling no more a concern.

Now she felt soft wind greet her,
A smiling song on her face.
Brave wheels went around and around,
As though she were first in a race.

Sweet rhythm of pedals spinning,
Warm whirr of rubber on road.
Brave wheels went around and around,
At last, at the end she slowed.

With a glad sigh, she turned back
And guided her steed for home.
Brave wheels went around and around,
Sunlight sparkling on chrome.

Make Connections

How does the writer help you to understand how the girl feels in "Sunlight Sparkling on Chrome"?
ESSENTIAL QUESTION

How do Jerome in *Try, Try Again* and the girl in "Sunlight Sparkling on Chrome" achieve their goals? **TEXT TO TEXT**

Focus on Literary Elements

Repetition Repeating a word or a phrase makes readers slow down and take notice. This encourages readers to focus on the meaning of the words.

Repetition also helps a poet achieve a rhythm that matches the meaning of the words, actions, or feelings he or she is expressing.

Read and Find In "Sunlight Sparkling on Chrome," the repetition of the line "Brave wheels went around and around" helps us understand what the rider feels. The poet uses these words to show that the rider feels brave. When the poem is read aloud, the use of the repeated line along with the rhythm and rhyme pattern in each verse gives a sense of the bicycle wheels moving.

Your Turn

Work with a group to create a multimedia version of the poem. Read the poem aloud several times until you can feel the rhythm. Make an audio recording of the poem. Then create a soundtrack or a series of drawings to accompany the recording.